Meditative Coloring Book 4:

HEARTS

Aliyah Schick

Sacred Imprints

Other Books by Aliyah Schick

- *Mary Magdalene's Words: Two Women's Spiritual Journey, Both Truth and Fiction, Both Ancient and Now.*
- *Meditative Coloring Book 1: Angels*
- *Meditative Coloring Book 2: Crosses*
- *Meditative Coloring Book 3: Ancient Symbols*
- *Meditative Coloring Book 5: Labyrinths*
- *Finally, a Book of Poetry by Aliyah Schick*

ISBN: 978-0-9844125-1-8

(c) 2008 Aliyah Schick

Table of Contents

> Dedicated to
> peaceful moments,
> open hearts,
> and
> self-discovery.

from my heart
to yours,
Aliyah

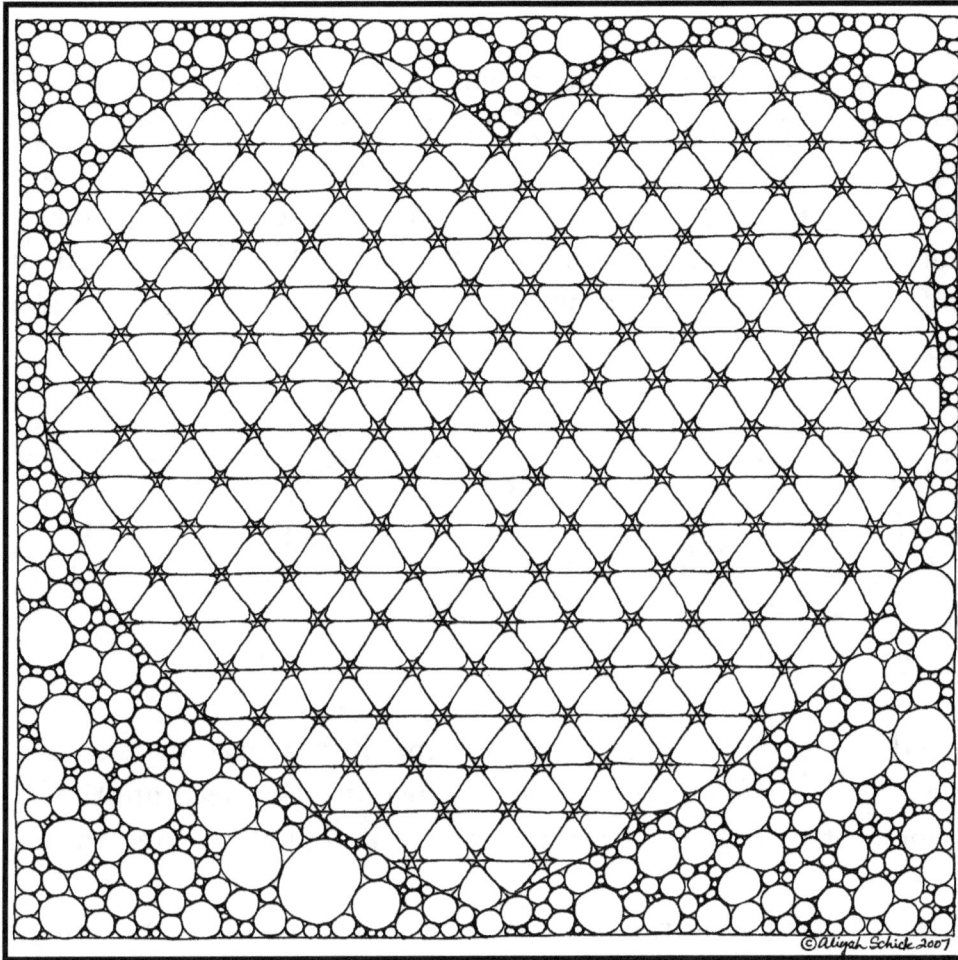

What Are Sacred Imprints™?

Each of these original pen-and-ink drawings is a unique work of art created through spiritual guidance by artist/healer Aliyah Schick. Every drawing of the Hearts Series began with a simple heart shape, then elaborated and varied in their own way, each ended up completely different from the others. In the *Sacred Imprints*™ *Meditative Coloring Book: Hearts* these drawings serve to inspire deeply meaningful meditative or prayerful experiences through the contemplative application of color.

The Heart as Symbol Throughout History

The earliest example of heart-shaped symbols we know of are stylized, heart-shaped fig leaves painted on a clay goblet from nearly 5,000 years ago, now in the Museum of Kabul in Afghanistan. Pottery from ancient Crete was decorated 4,000 years ago with ivy leaves shaped like hearts. Minoan palace frescoes used ivy vines and heart-shaped flowers and leaves. Corinthian vases from the 8th century B.C.E. show similar vines and leaves as well as heart-shaped grapes.

Heart-shaped ivy leaves on ancient Greek and Roman pottery represented eternal love as well as physical love. Ivy was also used to decorate the graves of Greeks and Romans, then Christians, symbolizing love beyond the grave.

In the 12th and 13th centuries the heart became a symbol of compassion and devotion in both religious and secular art. Ivy leaves were then used in paintings of love scenes, eventually painted in red, the color of blood, itself a symbol of love, good luck, and health since prehistory.

In Medieval times the traditions of knights and the literature of courtly love in central Europe transformed the leaf into our modern red heart, and developed its association with romance. When the red heart became one of the suits in playing cards in the 15th century its appearance in the art of the times spread rapidly, and it came to be commonly used as a symbol of spiritual and physical love.

In the 17th century Saint Margaret Mary Alocoque had a vision of the modern heart shape surrounded by thorns. This was named the "Sacred Heart of Jesus," suggesting love and devotion, and a worldwide Sacred Heart movement led by Jesuit priests spread the popularity of the symbol even further. The heart on a coat of arms during the Renaissance and Baroque periods stood for eternal faithfulness and courage.

Now the image of the heart declares love everywhere we look...in folk art, fine art, and commercial art, chocolate candies, note cards, bumper stickers, refrigerator magnets, and even the shape of honeymoon hotel beds and the occasional swimming pool. Our familiar red, stylized heart speaks a universal language around the world and down through the ages. Despite its being so common, the heart image still arouses feelings of love, caring, loyalty, and devotion. It is one of our favorite symbols.

Interesting Heart Image Trivia

- Early medical illustrations represented the human heart as a pine cone or a pyramid. Then from the 13th to 16th centuries they used the ivy leaf, upside down with the tip pointed slightly to the left and the stem indicating the arteries. Leonardo da Vinci used the inverted ivy leaf in his early anatomy sketches.
- The back and wings of a dove form a heart shape. Doves are linked to Aphrodite, Greek Goddess of Love.
- Mathematical formula for graphing a heart shape: $(x^2 + y^2 - 1)^3 = x^2 + y^3$
- The emoticon for typing a heart symbol (on its side) is <3 (less than, 3).

Suggestions for How to Use This Book

Use this *Sacred Imprints* ™ *Meditative Coloring Book* for spiritual connection, prayer, relaxation, healing, centering, and for coming into your deep, true self. You may simply wish to experience the images in quiet contemplation. Or, you may focus on a prayer or affirmation as you work with colors. You may ask for understanding regarding an issue you are dealing with. You may ask for a clearer sense of some aspect of yourself and how it serves you. You may wish to learn about your path or purpose in this lifetime.

Open your heart and your mind as you use this *Sacred Imprints* ™ *Meditative Coloring Book*. Pay attention to impressions and ideas, feelings, intuition, and messages. They may very well be exactly what you need to hear.

Tools
Choose your favorite coloring tools, or you might like to gather a variety of pens, crayons, colored pencils, chalk, oil pastels, markers, glitter pens, paints, etc. You may want to place a blank sheet of paper behind the page so ink or paint does not go through.

Music
Consider playing soft instrumental or contemplative background music.

Nature
Sometimes a favorite spot outdoors provides just the right environment for creative expression. Beach, woods, backyard, porch, treehouse, mountain top, stream, pond, park, etc.

Silence
You may prefer quiet, so that all your attention focuses on what you are doing. Emptiness can give rise to profound experience.

Meditation
You may like to meditate first, and then begin working with the colors. Try any of the many ways of meditation, or simply be with your breath for a few minutes, following it in and out. Or, you may wish to try the following meditation. Read it silently or out loud, slowly, pausing to draw in each breath.

Meditation

Take in a breath... and on the exhale release the day's happenings, settling into this peaceful time of creative, spiritual connection.

Take in a breath... and on the exhale let go of worries and troubles and burdens. You can pick them up again later if you need to.

Take in a breath... and on the exhale come into the center of your Self. From there drop a line down through your body, through the chair and the floor and into the earth. Through soil and sand and stone, through coal and underground stream, and minerals and precious metals. Down through all the colors and textures and densities of the earth, down into the hot magma at this planet's core. Down to the very center of the earth, to the Heart of the Mother. Tie your line there. Anchor yourself there.

Take in a breath... and on the exhale extend your line up from your center, through your body and out the crown of your head, up through the ceiling, the roof, and into the sky. Past clouds and wind and thinning gases, out through the atmosphere and into space. Past the sun and galaxy and stars and universe, out to the depths of the Source of All That Is. Feel your connection there. You are part of the great cosmos. You are one with all being.

Take in a breath... and on the exhale return to the drawing before you and ask that you be open to receiving guidance and understanding as you spend time with it. Know that there are no mistakes, only new choices and combinations and patterns that suggest new perception at an other-than-conscious level. Or that remind us of something that can now be released. Or that create an opening to new possibilities.

Take in a breath... and on the exhale release "shoulds" and rules and expectations. Let go and open to new possibilities.

Now, begin by picking up whatever color catches your attention.

About the Artist

Aliyah Schick has been an artist all of her life. After Peace Corps in the Andes Mountains of South America, she studied art full time for four years, then created and sold pottery and ceramic art pieces for many years. Later Aliyah worked in fiber and fabric, making soft sculptural wall pieces and art quilts, then fabric dolls designed to carry healing energy. Now she draws and paints, and she writes poems and prose.

At the heart of all this, Aliyah's real work is healing. She is a skilled and dynamic deep energetic healer. Her work in the multidimensional layers and patterns of the auric field is powerful and effective. The *Sacred Imprints* ™ and the *Meditative Coloring* ™ *Books* emerged as new expressions of Aliyah's healing work. Experiencing these drawings serves to remind us who we are, where we come from, and why we are here.

Aliyah lives and works in the beautiful Blue Ridge Mountains of North Carolina, where the energy of the earth is easily accessible, ancient, motherly, and obvious. A place where people speak with familiarity and reverence of the land and spirit, and where the sacred comes to sit with us on the porch to share the afternoon sun.

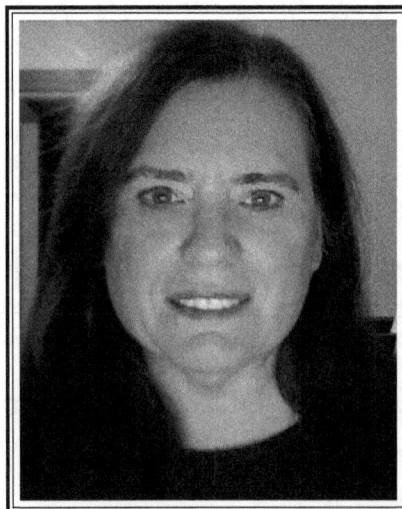

The
Drawings

Opposite each drawing is a blank page labeled
Meditative Impressions. Use these pages to catch
and keep hold of your thoughts, wishes, intentions,
affirmations, prayers, poems, memories, notes,
drawings, or whatever comes to you as you explore
coloring with this book. Make it yours.

11

Meditative Impressions

13

Meditative Impressions

14

15

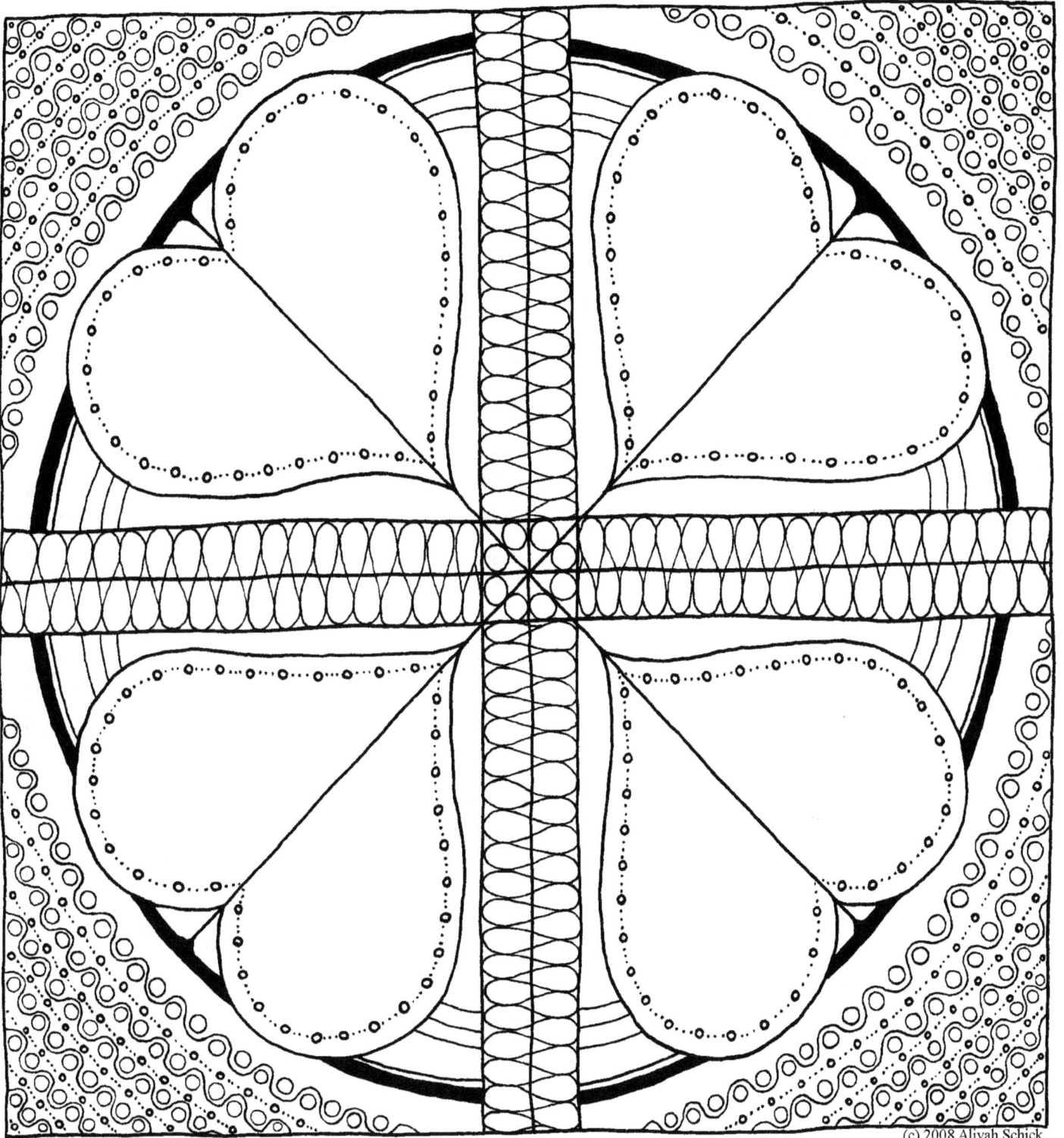

17

Meditative Impressions

(c) 2008 Aliyah Schick

Meditative Impressions

20

21

23

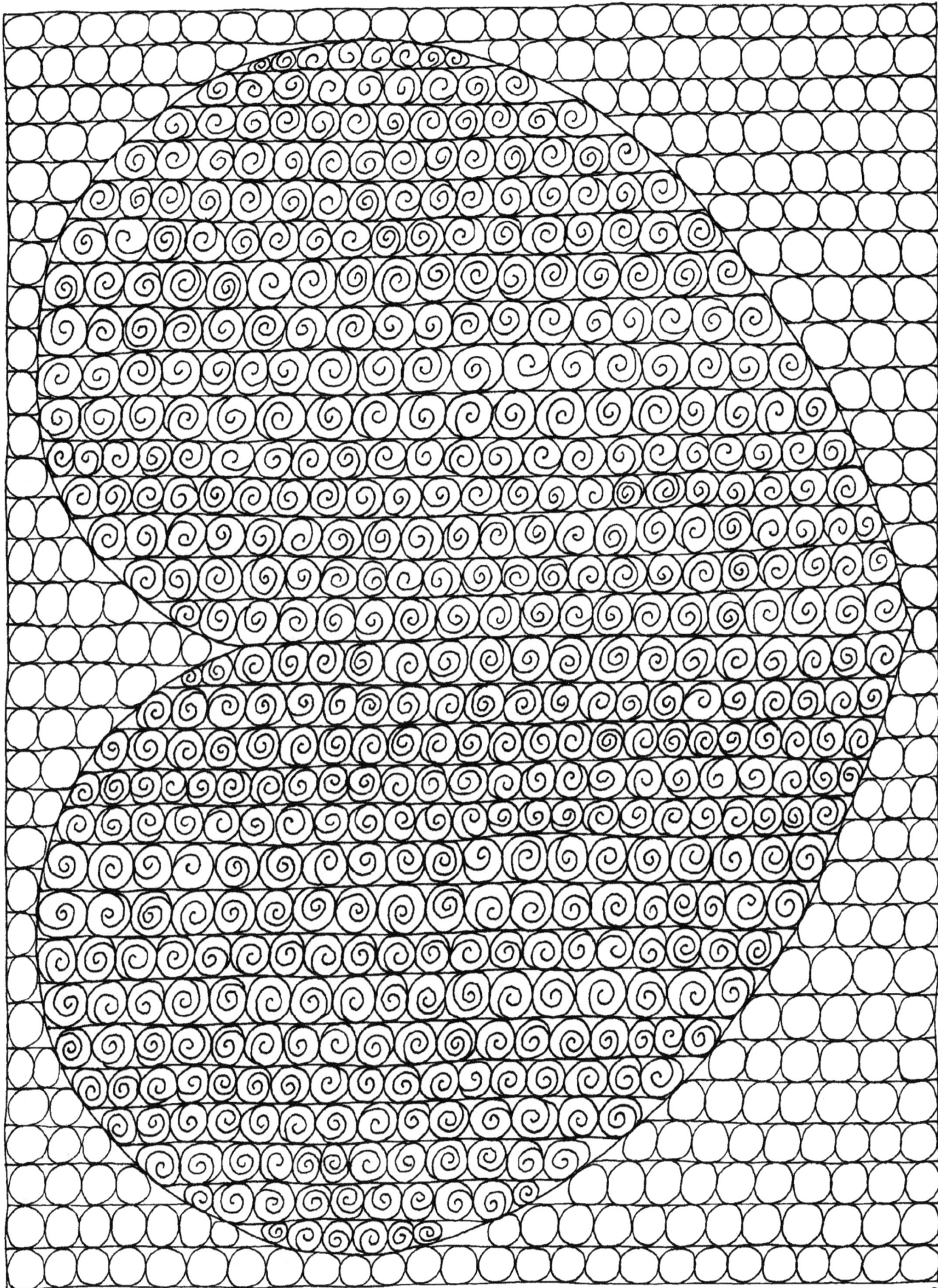

Meditative Impressions

Meditative Impressions

28

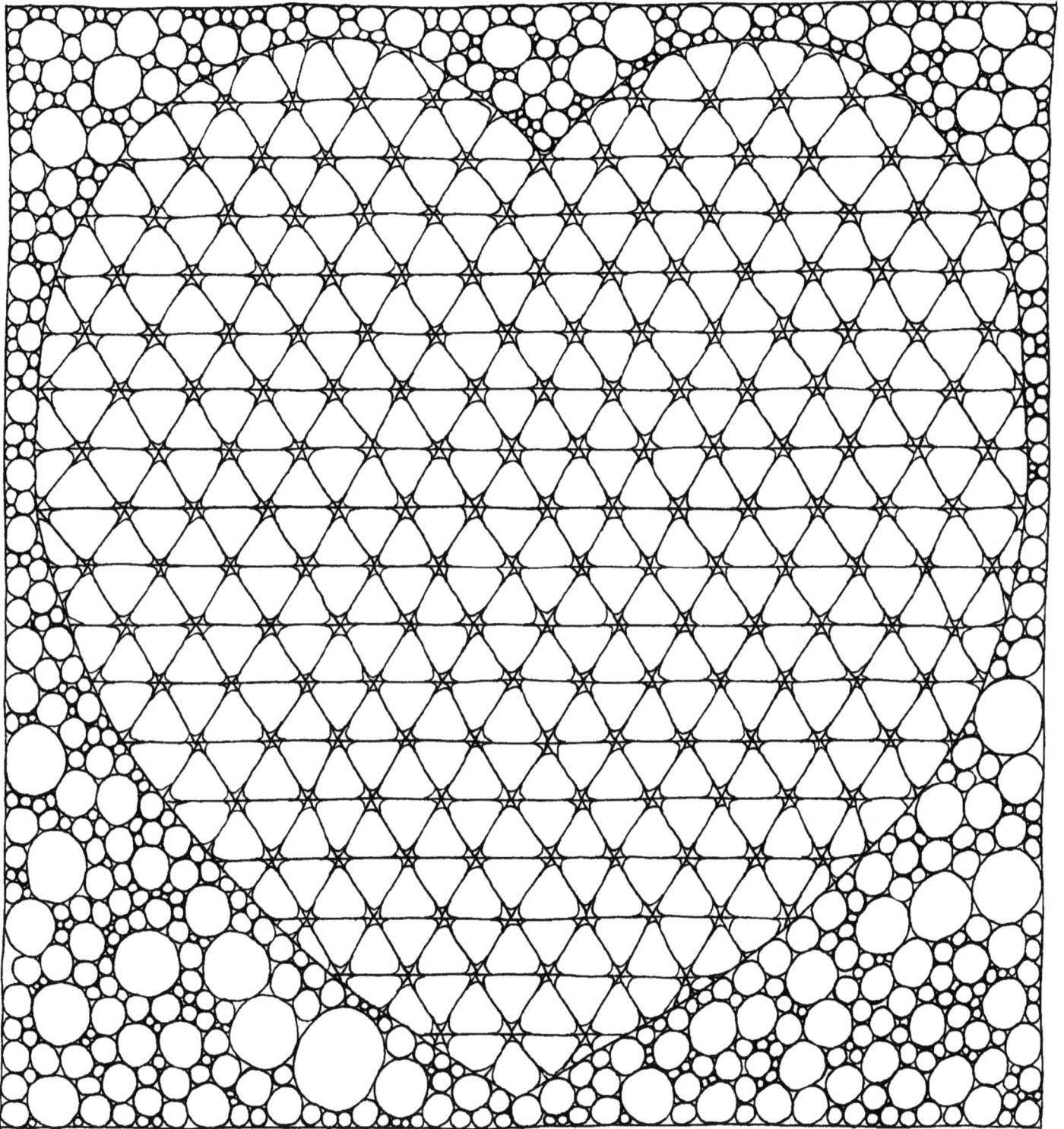

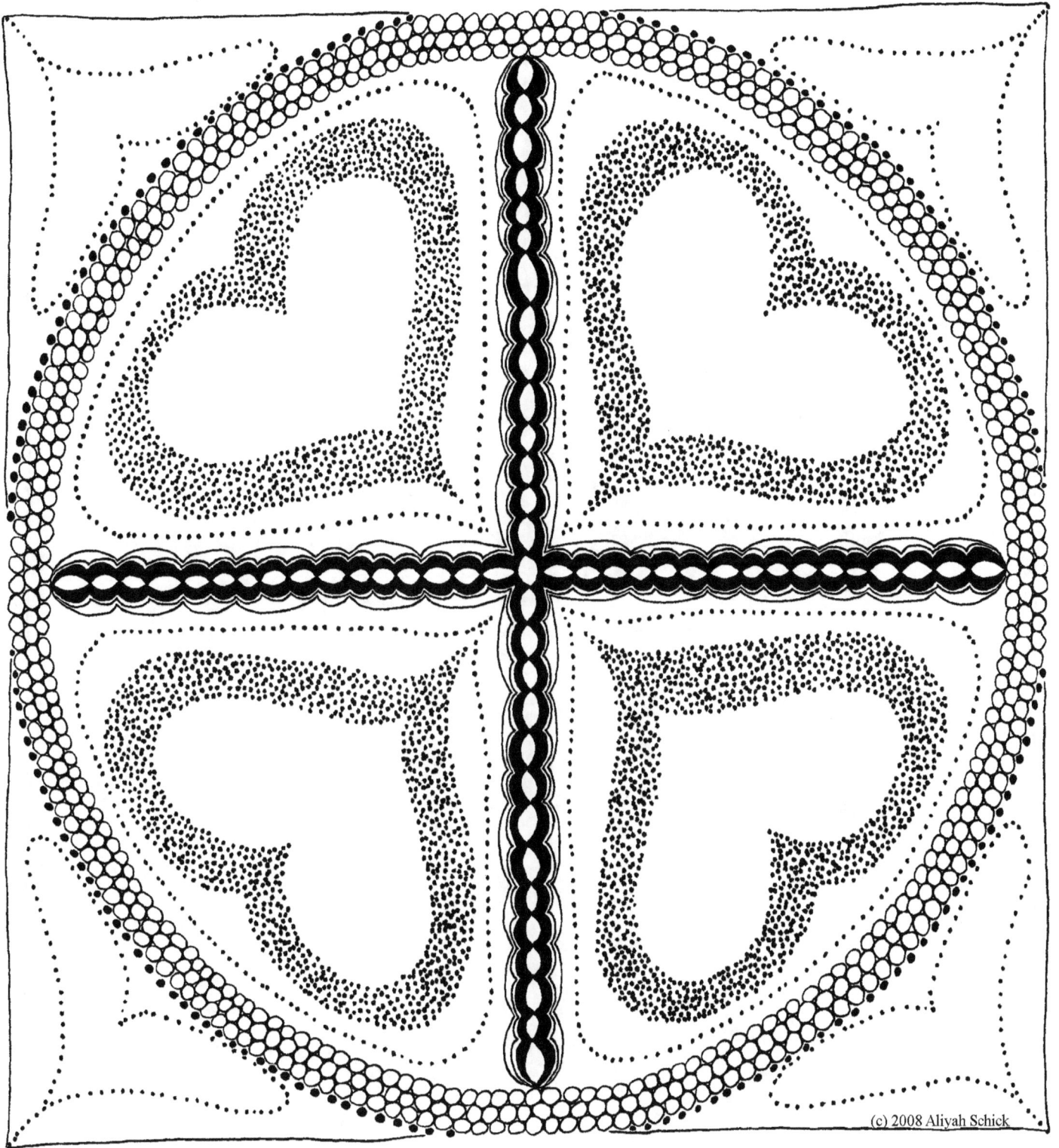

31

Meditative Impressions

33

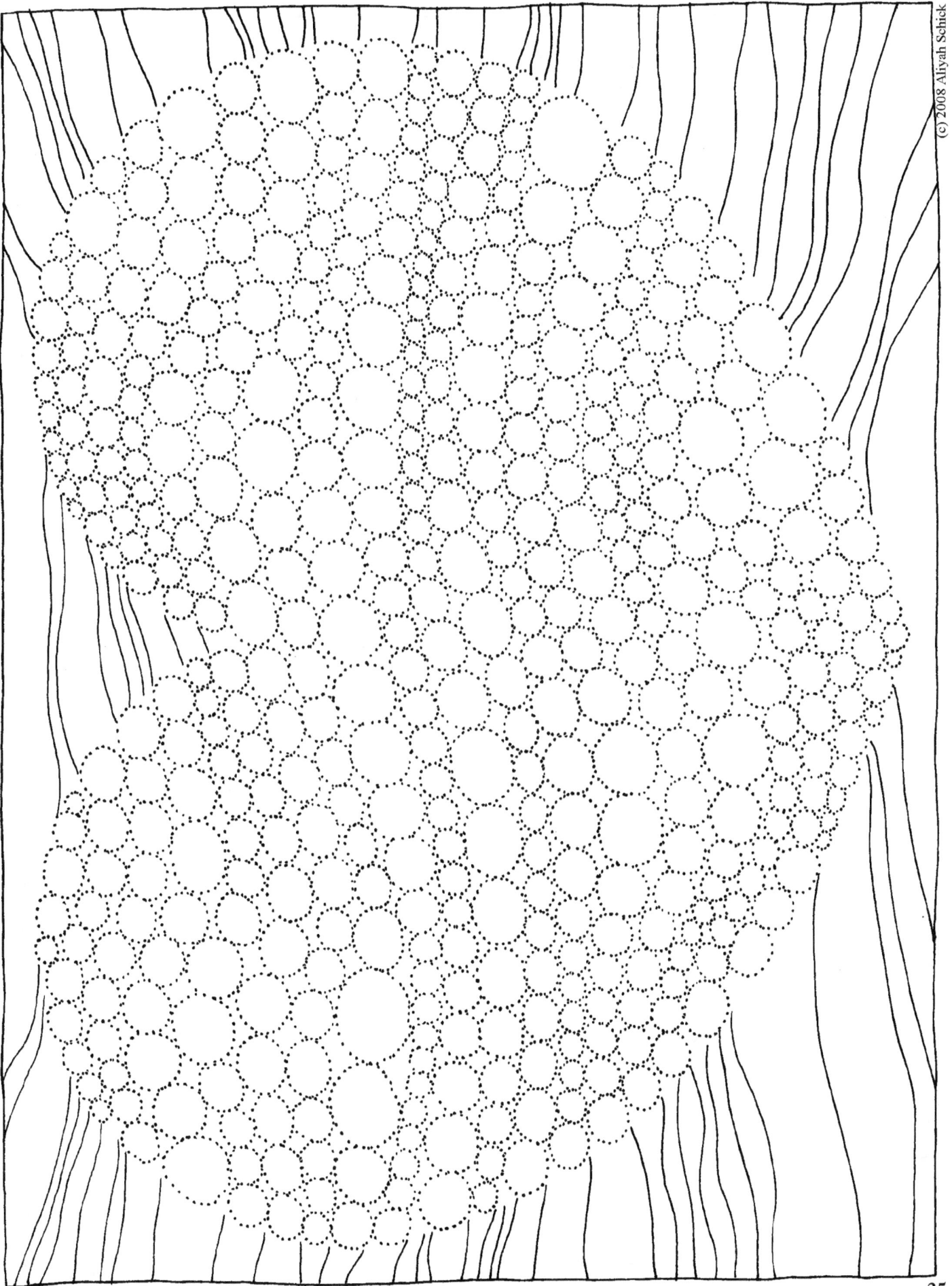

35

Meditative Impressions

41

43

45

Meditative Impressions

46

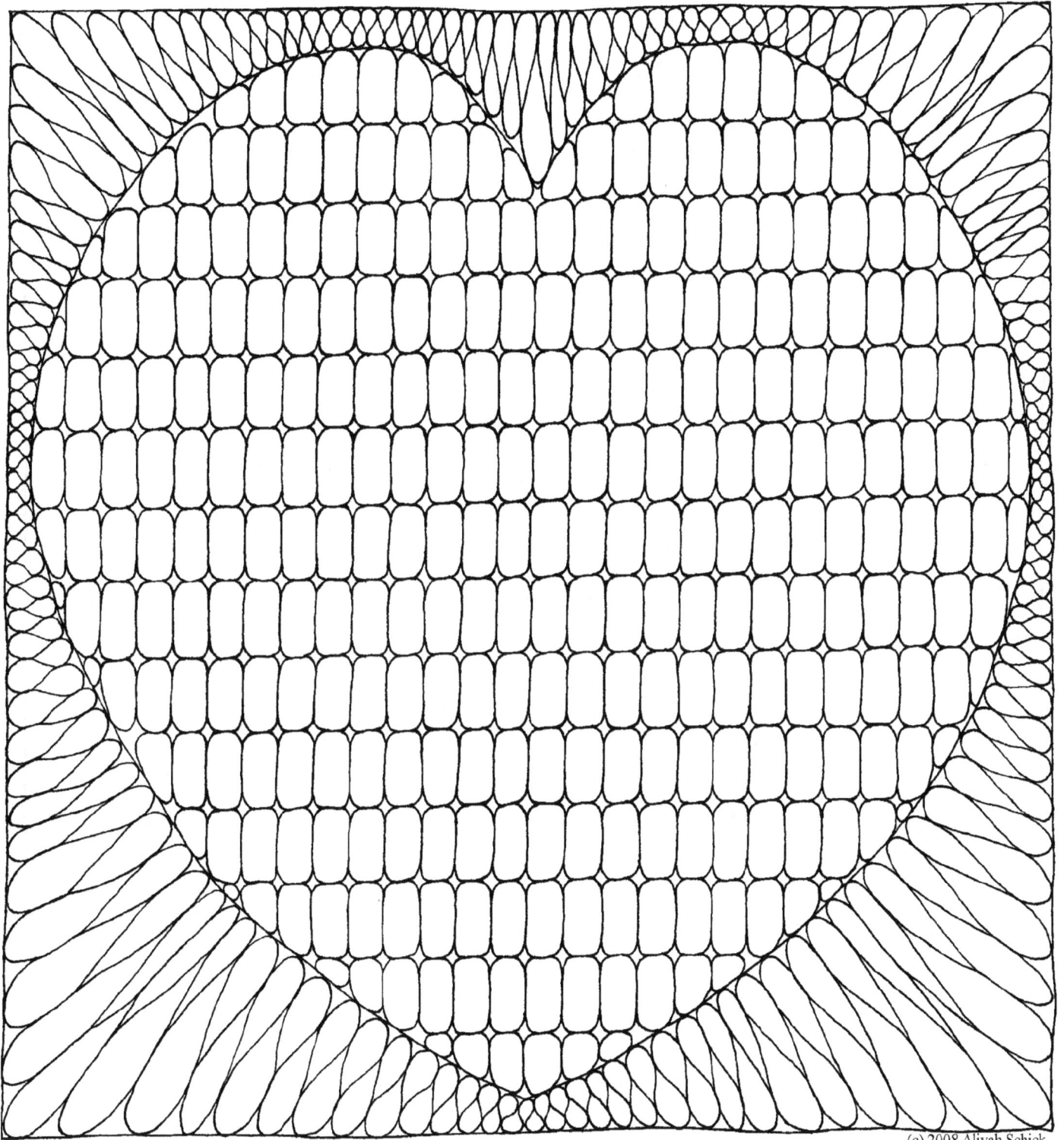

47

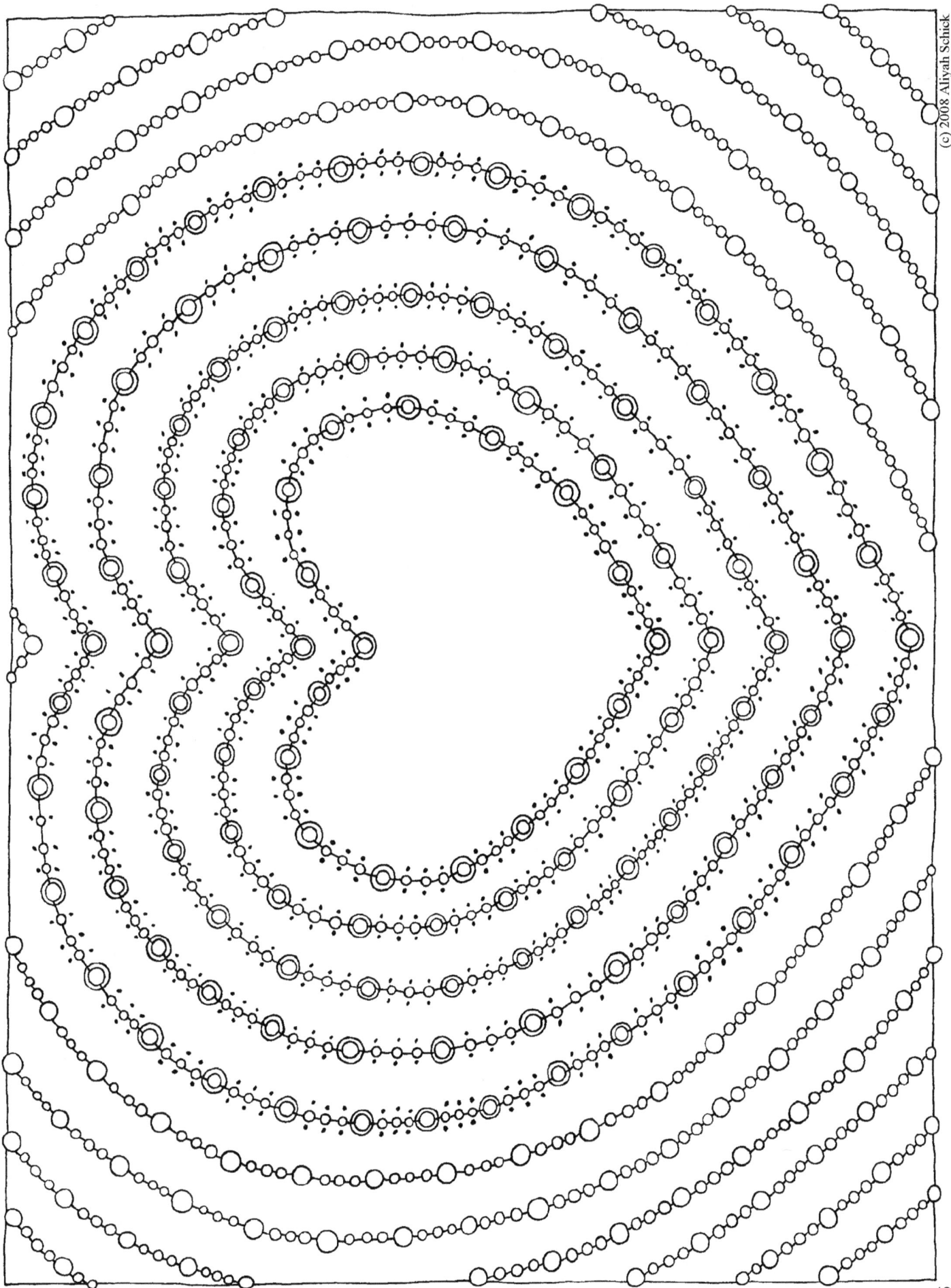

49

51

Meditative Impressions

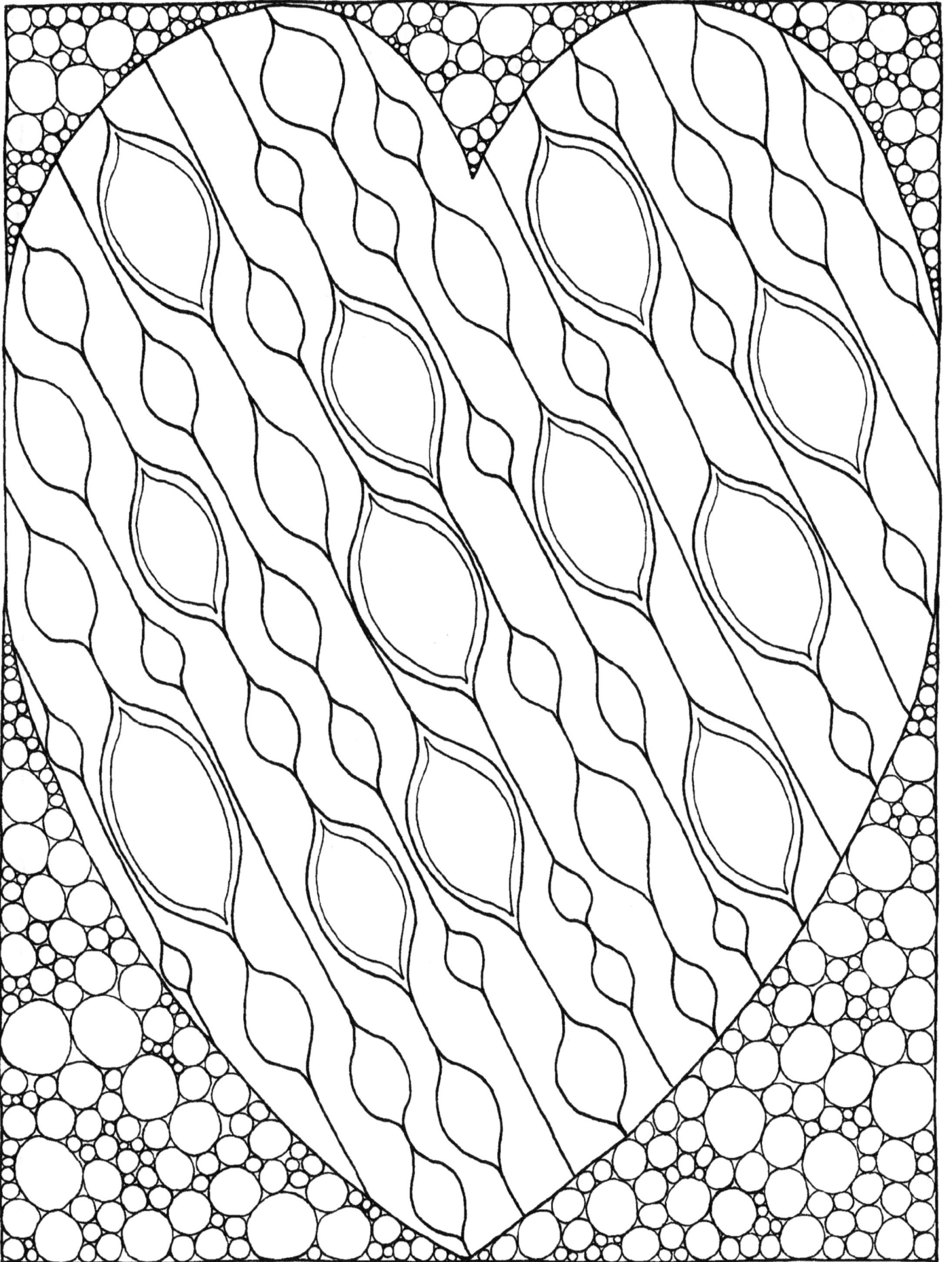

55

(c) 2008 Aliyah Schick

57

59

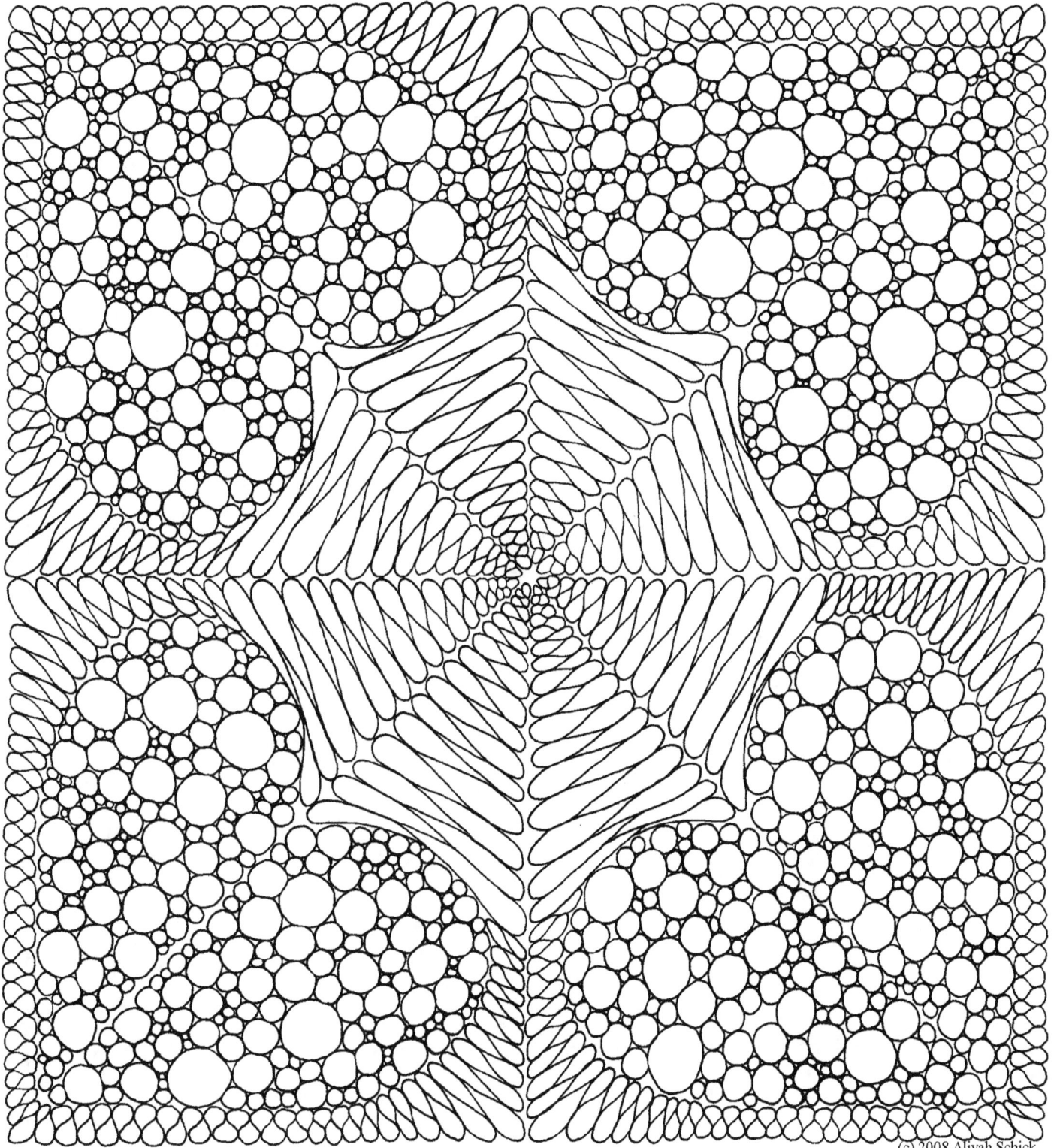

61

Meditative Impressions

62

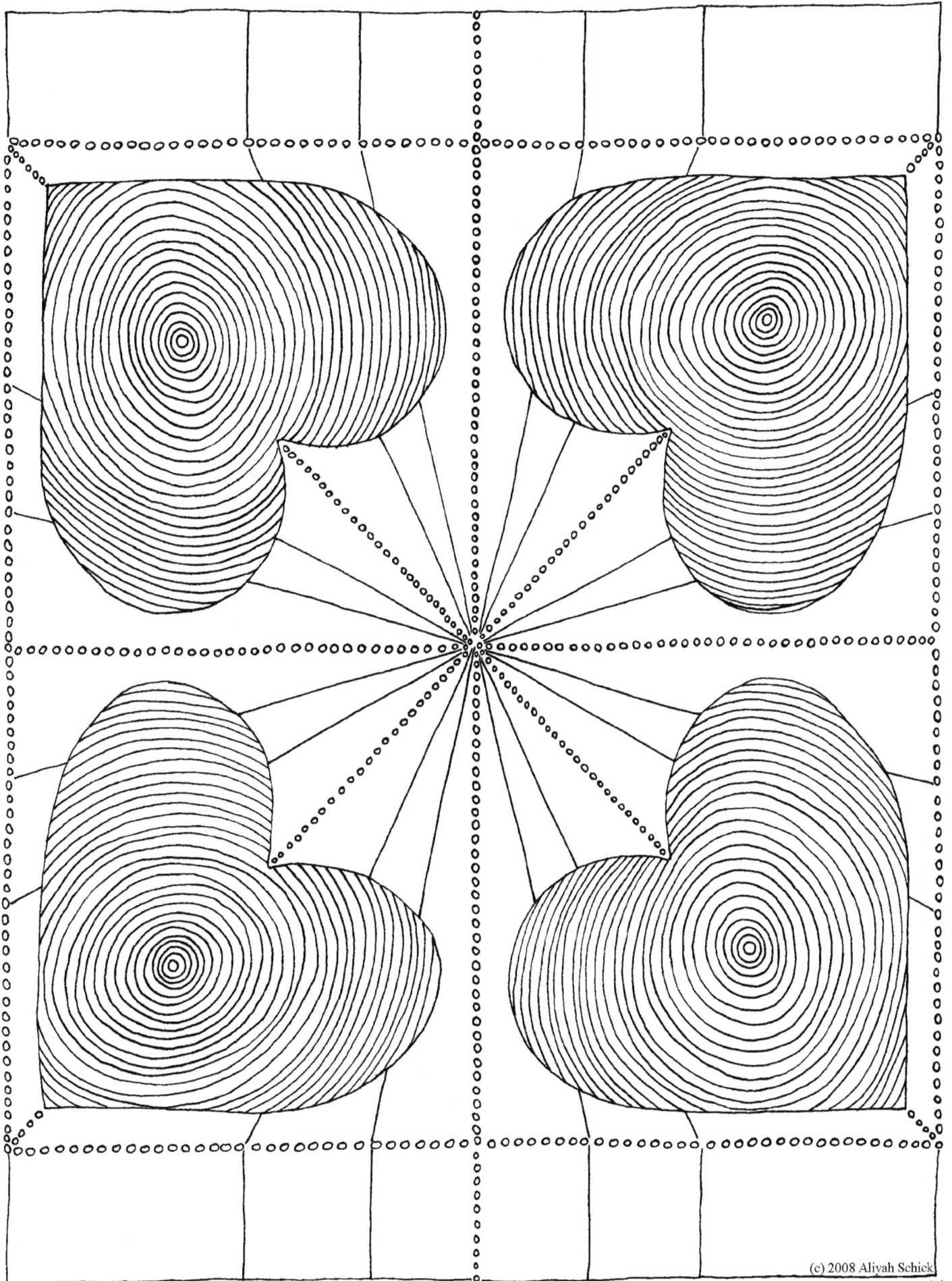

65

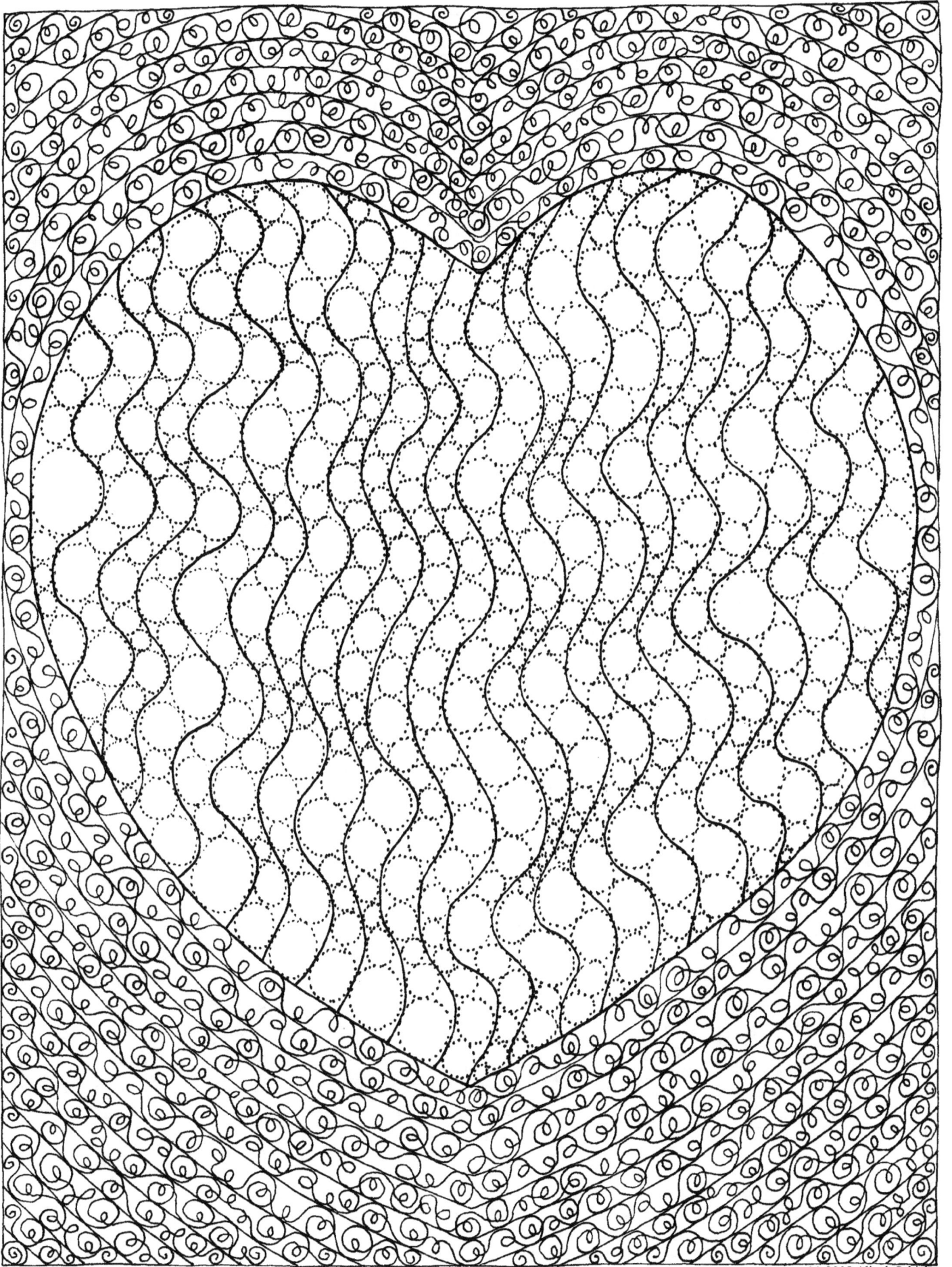

69

71

Meditative Impressions

Meditative Impressions

74

(c) 2008 Aliyah Schick

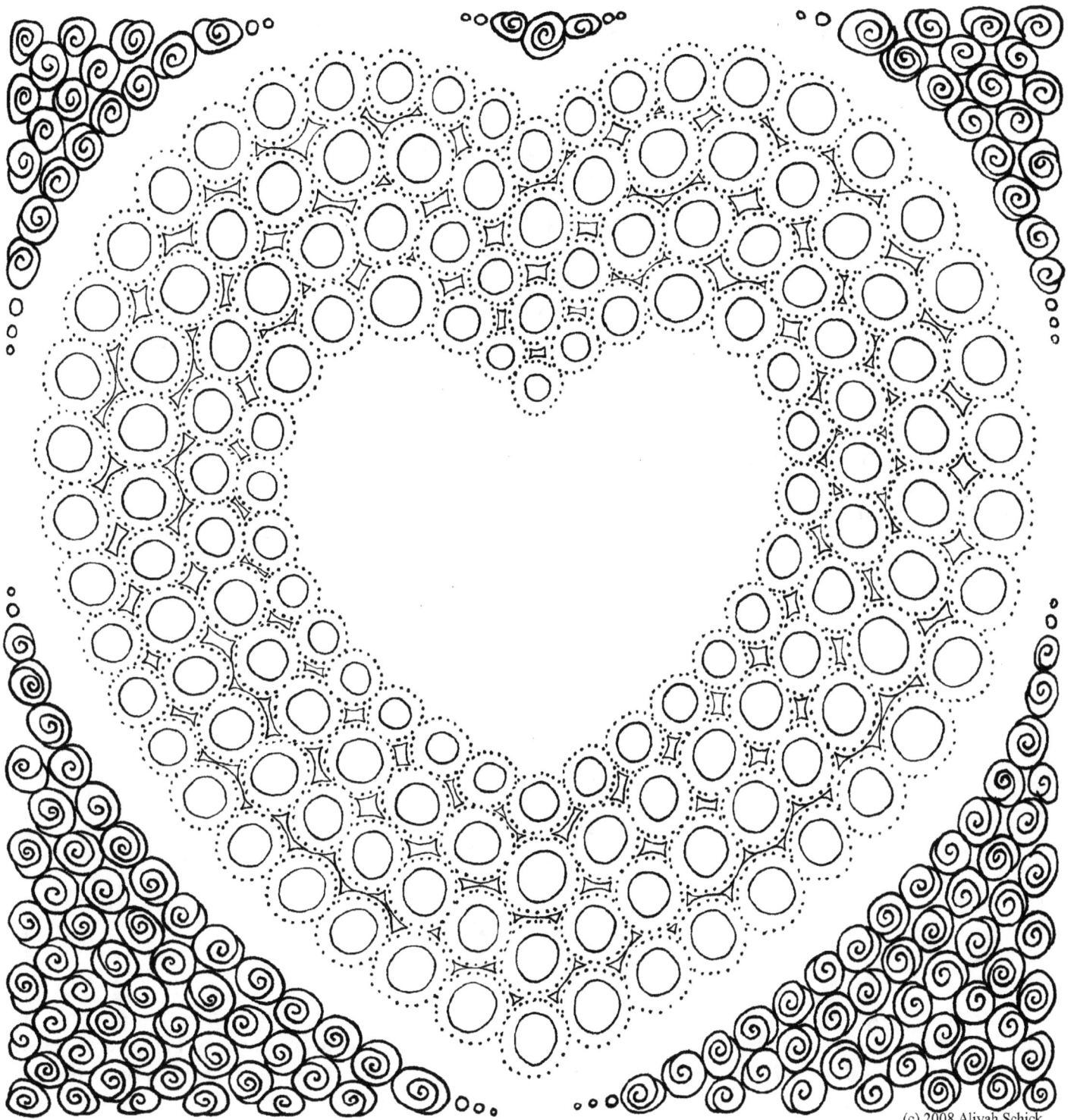

The Sacred Imprints™ Meditative Coloring Books
Five Volumes: Angels, Crosses, Ancient Symbols, Hearts, and Labyrinths

---

<u>Meditative Coloring Book 1 -- Angels</u>

The Sacred Imprints ™ Angelic images are drawn during a centering meditation. With a pen in each hand, Aliyah allows the lines to go where they will, the two sides mirroring each other. Every movement is guided by spirit; every drawing is different; and each one is a wonderful surprise filled with angelic presence.

<u>Meditative Coloring Book 2 -- Crosses</u>

The cross is one of our most ancient and enduring sacred symbols, found in nearly every culture throughout human existence. It symbolizes the celestial, spirtual divine coming into being in this material world. It represents God taking form, and the integration of soul into physical life. The drawings of the Crosses Series feature ancient and contemporary images of the cross in reflections of the deep spiritual significance of its form.

Meditative Coloring Book 3 -- Ancient Symbols

Ancient and indigenous sacred images speak deeply to us, to our bellies and our bones, to our cellular memory and our wisdom, to our souls' yearnings. Native peoples throughout time and place see the sacred in all of life. For them, holiness is life and life is holiness. Life is the manifestation of the holy in all things. The drawings of the Ancient Symbols Series feature timeless designs used by every culture on earth to remind us of the sacred.

Meditative Coloring Book 4 -- Hearts

The heart is one of our favorite symbols, evoking feelings of love, caring, loyalty, and devotion. As you spend time with these Sacred Imprints Heart drawings, open your heart to live with more compassion for others and for yourself. Open your life to deeper connection with the earth and all of life. Open yourself to recognize the sacred in all things, including in yourself.

Meditative Coloring Book 5 -- Labyrinths

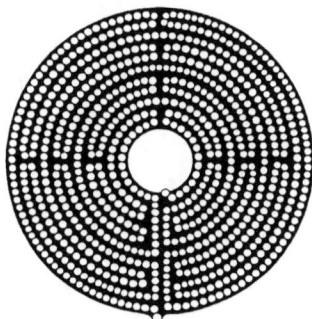

These original artist's labyrinth drawings invite you to color your steps into the labyrinth, one by one, as you contemplate, meditate, or pray. Go deep into your inner wisdom and guidance where questions' answers reveal themselves and choices come clear. Or simply relax and be with your breathing. Now you can bring your labyrinth with you to wherever you need to be.

Sacred Imprints